50 Brilliant PE Challenges

Using Just a

Hoop

Will Hussey

Brilliant
PUBLICATIONS

We hope you and your pupils enjoy using the ideas in this book. Listed below are a few of our other books which might be of interest to you. Information on these and all our other books can be found on our website: www.brilliantpublications.co.uk.

Other books in the series

50 Brilliant PE Challenges Using Just a Beanbag
50 Brilliant PE Challenges Using Just a Tennis Ball

Other PE books

100+ Fun Ideas for Teaching PE Games
43 Team-building Activities for KS1
43 Team-building Activities for KS2
100+ Fun Ideas for Playground Games

Other books written by Will Hussey

Where Can an Elephant Hide?
Where Can an Elephant Roost?
Brilliant Activities to Stimulate Creative Thinking

Published by Brilliant Publications
Unit 10
Sparrow Hall Farm
Edlesborough
Dunstable
Bedfordshire
LU6 2ES, UK

www.brilliantpublications.co.uk

The name Brilliant Publications and the logo are registered trademarks.

Written by Will Hussey
Illustrations and cover illustration by Martha Hardy

Contents

Introduction

50 Brilliant PE Challenges Using Just a Hoop does exactly what it says on the tin.

This handy teacher resource will provide a wealth of active and enjoyable activities, inspiring outstanding learning with minimal preparation.

A mixture of differentiated individual, group and whole class activities, with suggestions for further challenge and extension, ensures the busy teacher can create bespoke lessons.

The **50 Brilliant PE Challenges** series of books believes less is more: inclusive competition and engagement facilitated by minimal preparation and resources regardless of subject expertise. Brilliant challenges create brilliant PE lessons!

Key

	Individual challenge
	Group/paired challenge
	Whole class challenge
	Moderate difficulty
	Intermediate
	Advanced

1. Rock 'n' Roll

> **Challenge**
>
> Can the children 'master' their hoop?
> Encourage them to explore rolling their hoop in
> different directions, sending them to pre-determined
> positions on a clock face.

Tip

Working with a friend can provide a positional target, aiding
focus and accuracy.

Development

Suggest different numbers for the children to 'aim' at, awarding
a score appropriate to their level of accuracy.

2. Straight forward

Challenge

The aim is to roll the hoop along a straight line pathway, deviating as little as possible for as far as possible.

Tip
The most successful course is typically achieved by using a firmly weighted launch.

Development
Two or more children can roll their hoops simultaneously, endeavouring to maintain a parallel course.

3. Wrist watch

Challenge

Children attempt to rotate the hoop around one wrist before seamlessly transferring it to the other arm.

Tip
Centrifugal force dictates that the faster the hoop rotates the harder it is to control.

Development
Try rotating more than one hoop at a time, or see how far a hoop can be transferred along a human chain in this manner.

4. Sculpture

> **Challenge**
>
> Ask children to strike a pose in which they can carefully balance a hoop; encourage them to be as creative as possible.

Tip
Pupils should try and hold their balances still for a suitable amount of time. They can always work with a friend to help them position their hoop.

Development
Create a sequence of hoop balances to fluently progress through.

S. Hula's who?

Challenge

The children endeavour to continually rotate the hoops by gyrating their hips.

Tip
It's most definitely all in the hips; those wearing too many clothing layers may find it difficult to communicate the required action.

Development
Some children can rotate more than one hoop at a time, or simultaneously manage to travel from one place to another.

6. Skip it

The children should try to complete consecutive skips by stepping or jumping through their continuously turning hoop.

Tip
Running forwards whilst stepping through the hoop seems to be the preferred action. Ensure individuals select a hoop that is large enough to step through.

Development
Challenge the children further by suggesting they try turning the hoop backwards as well as forwards.

7. Foot loose

Challenge

Requiring balance, coordination and agility, the children should aim to stand on one leg whilst rotating the hoop around the other foot.

Tip
Children tend to instinctively select the smallest hoops for this task, necessitating unsustainable leg speed; medium-sized hoops are typically the best to use.

Development
Try rotating more than one hoop at a time, perhaps using the arms in addition to the leg.

8. Contortion

Challenge

Children should try to weave their way in and out of a stationary hoop in a figure-of-eight pattern whilst holding it vertically. The hoop must be held still and in contact with the ground at all times.

Tip
'Feet-first' seems to be the favoured approach. Children should consider carefully at what point to swap hands.

Development
Try a different sized hoop. See how quickly the challenge can be completed or race against a friend.

9. Back spin

Challenge

Encourage the children to dispatch the hoop using back-spin; can they deploy sufficient skill for the hoop to return to the starting point?

Tip
It's most definitely 'all in the wrist'; children should focus on achieving backwards spin rather than distance.

Development:
Vary the size of hoop used, and consider the contrast between different playing surfaces. Whose hoop is the most 'obedient?'

10. Flaming hoop

Children roll their hoops in to a space. Can they manage to climb through the hoop before it falls flat to the floor?

Tip
Rolling the hoop firmly in a straight line makes it easier to get into position. Pupils should step through the hoop – not dive!

Development
Try negotiating the hoop without even touching it. Alternatively, children may ask a friend to roll the hoop in a direction of their choice.

11. Wrap around

The children stand back-to-back and pass a hoop around the outside of them both as many times as they can in a given time limit.

Challenge

Tip
Use both hands to collect and pass the hoop. Keeping both feet planted firmly on the floor whilst rotating the hips appears to be the most effective technique.

Development
Challenge the children to both turn the same way (clockwise for instance), requiring increased agility, coordination and cooperation.

12. Pit stop

Challenge

The children compete in relay teams to negotiate a 'tyre' obstacle course; ensuring one foot is placed in to every hoop.

Tip
Keeping the knees high and looking ahead curbs forward rotation.

Development
Place the hoops a wider distance apart, ensuring a running action can still be maintained.

13. Twister

Challenge

Compete in small groups to see whose hoop can spin for the longest before falling flat.

Tip
Playing on harder, smoother surfaces increases the potential spinning time.

Development
Children compete consecutively within teams, vying to see which team will have 'the last hoop standing'.

Challenge

Pupils take it in turns to outwit their opponent, using their friends as playing pieces. The crosses should indicate such by folding their arms in front of their chest. As is customary, the winner is the first to achieve three in a row.

Tip
The winner of the previous game should contest the next, although their new opponent has the opportunity of playing first. In the event of a draw, two new players are selected.

Development
Insist that players have a short time limit in which to make their moves.

15. Whose hoop?

Challenge

Children work with a partner to exchange their hoops as often as possible in a given time over a set distance.

Tip
This task works best with a gap of approximately five to ten metres; too short and the hoop lacks the power required to roll directly, too far and the hoop has insufficient momentum.

Development
After using their preferred hand, stipulate that they use the other arm.

16. Hoop's first?

> **Challenge**
>
> Children race in teams to see who can be the first to cover a set distance. They must roll the hoops; carrying is not allowed. Players must wait for the hoop to fall flat to the ground before rolling it again.

Tip
Inevitably, those who try to roll the hoop forcibly in order to cover the greatest distance go awry. Short, controlled pushes usually prove most effective, allowing individuals to maintain a direct course.

Development
Participants could try using their weaker hand or negotiate an irregular course.

17. Stepping stones

Children work in teams to cross a 'swamp' by using their hoops as stepping stones. They should have one less hoop than the number of team members.

Challenge

Tip
Teams will typically place their hoops too far apart, leading to overbalancing and having to start again.

Development
Stipulating that the children must carry additional hoops as 'baggage' requires even greater teamwork and cooperation.

18. Three wheeling

Challenge

Work together with a partner to complete a course in 'three-legged' fashion, linked together by a hoop around adjacent ankles.

Tip
A certain amount of outward pressure is required to keep the hoop in position. Use smaller hoops initially.

Development
Challenge pupils to use more than one hoop to join together, or even two hoops of different sizes!

19. Venn game

Challenge

The children take turns to throw their hoop, attempting to be the first to overlap their opponent's hoop.

Tip
This can be a very tactical game; deciding when to throw for the win or when to merely play safe requires careful consideration.

Development
Curtail the size of the playing area to change the dynamics of the game. Introduce a joker (effectively a 'double throw') a player can choose to use at one point.

20. Foot loops

Challenge

Children compete in relay teams to be the fastest to complete a course, rotating the hoop around one ankle whilst running along.

Tip
The most successful teams are the ones who keep the hoop under control; a steady and controlled pace tends to beat a reckless speed-orientated approach.

Development
Each time a team member completes their leg they must throw their hoop onto an 'anchor' hoop before the next person can 'go.'

21. Drop zone

Challenge

Children work in pairs to see how many times they can pass the hoop over their bodies whilst standing back-to-back.

Tip
Embracing gravity often enables the activity to be completed more quickly; careful positioning and teamwork is what counts!

Development
Race other pairings to see who can be the first to reach a target goal. Alternatively introduce a time limit for children to challenge their own total. What effect does using hoops of different sizes (and partners) have?

22. Round zero

The children should develop a short routine consisting of three different balances utilising a hoop.

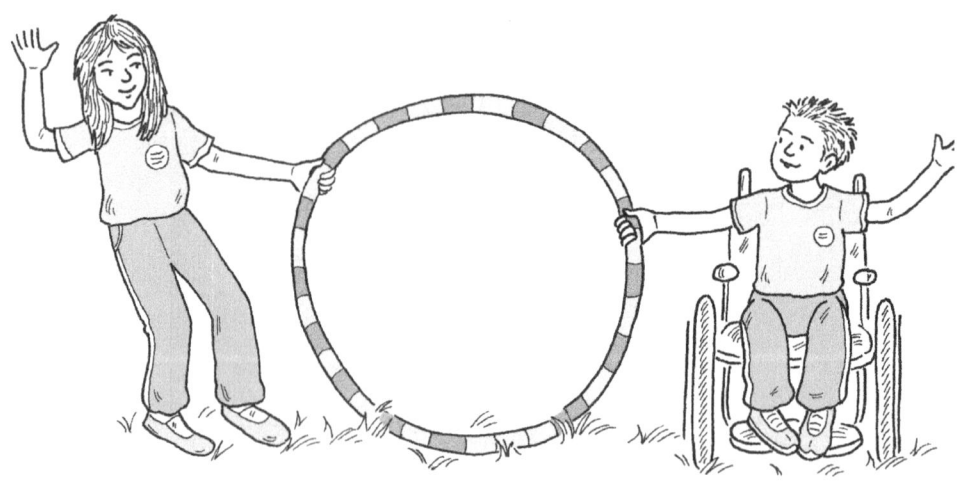

Tip
Suggesting that each balance should be at a different level helps to create contrast and variation.

Development
Extend the sequence of balances, collaborate with additional pupils or include an extra hoop.

23. Hoop scotch

Challenge

Children take it in turns to complete a course, alternatively hopping over and stepping into the pre-positioned hoops.

Tip
Children should complete out and back journeys, necessitating a change in direction midway.

Development
Compete relay-fashion against other teams to see who can complete the course the quickest. Extend and adapt the course to increase the level of challenge.

24. Shape shifter

Challenge

Children work in teams to create different shapes, letters or patterns when the teacher prompts them.

Tip

Children should take turns directing each design.

Development

Can the class work together to create 'the bigger picture' or even a word or phrase? Groups can take it in turns to demonstrate designs that the others then try to copy.

25. Labyrinth

Challenge

A team of children position their hoops at varying angles but at an accessible height. Team members take it in turns to try to climb through each hoop making as little contact as possible.

Tip
Stipulate that one edge of each hoop should be in contact with the ground to begin with, to provide stability and ensure they are positioned safely.

Development
Compete to see who can complete the course the quickest, adding extra time penalties for each contact made.

26. Stack's that

Children should work together to build the tallest structure possible, made solely from hoops.

Challenge

Tip
Using a variety of different-sized hoops seems to increase the number of potential design possibilities.

Development
Stipulate that a particular colour or size of hoop must be at the highest point of the structure.

27. Barrel roll

Challenge

Groups endeavour to transport their hoops along the line by using their feet only; if they drop one then it must return to the start.

Tip
Slow and steady wins the race. Children should keep their feet horizontal and allow the hoop to dangle down to help avoid the hoops slipping off.

Development
Try racing against another group or introducing a time limit. Alternatively, stipulate there must be a hoop's width between each participant.

28. Chain gang

Challenge

Children should try and create the longest chain possible that allows them to move as an efficient unit.

Tip

As with 'Three Wheeling' (page 22), it can take a little practice to work out an effective technique. Start with fewer links and gradually progress to adding extras.

Development

Award each team a points total prior to navigating a simple course. Penalise them every time the chain is broken.

29. Wigwam

Pupils creatively position their hoops to create a shelter surrounding a member of their group.

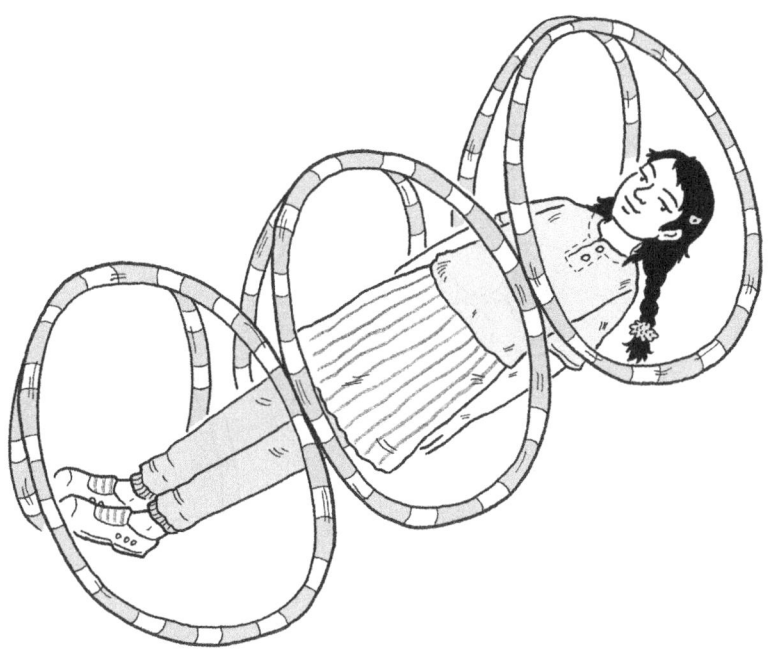

Tip
Members of the group may need to 'anchor' some of the hoops during the initial construction phase.

Development
Group members take it in turns to enter and exit their shelter without disturbing the wigwam.

30. Two-wheel drive

Children must link arms with a partner to travel in an agreed direction, each using their 'free' arm to roll a hoop along.

Tip
Success can only be achieved through close cooperation, rolling the hoops at the same time, in the same direction with a similar weighting.

Development
Stipulate the direction that the children should take, perhaps introducing some twists and turns.

31. Four-wheel drive

> **Challenge**
>
> Children must link arms as a foursome and travel in an agreed direction, the pair on the end of the line using their 'free' arms to roll a hoop along.

Tip
Rotate the positions of the children in the line. The 'core' pupils should coordinate the strategy and instruct those on the peripheries.

Development
Teams compete against each other, having to return to the starting point should they become detached.

---

32. Skittles

The class is split into two. Children take it in turns to roll their hoop at their classmates from an agreed position, endeavouring to score points by making contact. Each child has three goes and tries to accumulate the maximum points. The 'human skittles' should use their fingers to indicate how many points they are worth.

Tip
Ensure the hoops roll along the ground, remaining in contact at all times; throwing is not permitted. 'Skittles' stand inside grounded hoops, ensuring they remain in the same position.

Development
Reposition the skittles, altering distance and configuration accordingly.

33. Drop down

Challenge

The whole class are organised into four different teams. One child is sent to locate any one of eight different hoops. On finding a hoop, the child signals to their teammates; each team member must then step through the hoop before continuing on to find the next hoop. The winning team is the first to pass through all eight of the hoops.

Tip
Ensure the hoops are spaced well apart, ideally placed in locations not easily visible from another.

Development
Number each of the team members, and stipulate they have to pass through each of the hoops in order.

34. Loopy hoop

Challenge

Children stand in the middle of a 'home' hoop and note the colour. When the teacher calls that particular colour of hoop, those children should swap places with another member of the class with the same colour. When the teacher shouts 'Loopy hoop', everyone swaps places at the same time.

Tip
Ensure the area is large enough for the children to navigate safely.

Development
Children can run, skip, hop or move between their 'home' hoops in a variety of different ways. Alternatively the class can travel around the outside of the playing area.

35. Magpie

Challenge

The class compete in teams to see who can gather the most points, running relay-fashion to retrieve single hoops until none remain. Allocate points values for different sized/coloured hoops with one particular one worth double.

Tip
Most, but not all children, recognise it is beneficial to retrieve the highest value hoops first.

Development
Announce alternative points values for the hoops midway through the game, encouraging teams to adapt their strategy.

36. Inside out

> This is a whole class elimination game. Children **Challenge** are instructed to undertake a number of tasks focused around their hoop eg 'Complete ten star jumps with one foot placed inside and the other outside the hoop; the last person to complete is retired from the game.

Tip
Affiliate the children to a team according to the colour of their hoop.

Development
Children undertake tasks requiring them to swap hoops with another team member.

37. Hoop's who?

Children compete to be the last person in the class to be caught. One person starts the game as 'tag' and shouts an instruction to the rest of the class, such as "Anyone wearing red." Children who fit this criteria try to run from one side to the other without being tagged. Once tagged they join the person who is 'on'.

Tip

Participants should only run in the same direction; only when there are no children remaining on one side can they return in the opposite direction.

Development

Increase the parameters of the playing area. Introduce a forfeit that children should undertake upon being tagged before rejoining the game.

38. Blow out

> **Challenge**
>
> Spread out an area full of hoops. The class then have to compete in a game of tag but no one is allowed to step inside a hoop or they are eliminated from the game.

Tip
Ensure the playing area is plenty large enough and that the hoops are suitably well spaced out.

Development
Appoint an eliminated player to reposition some of the hoops midway through the game, ensuring the participants continue to tread carefully.

39. Duck, duck, hoop ☆

> ### Challenge
> Children sit in a circle of hoops. Choose one person to walk around the outside tapping each participant and repeating the word 'duck'. They signal one particular person by altering the word to 'hoop' before racing back 'home'. The chosen child gives chase and tries to return the tag before the instigator reaches his/her own hoop. The person who is 'it' initiates the next round.

Tip
Children should only be selected once until everyone has had a turn. Those who have already had a go should indicate by crossing their arms (or some other method).

Development
Increase the size of the circle, choose more than one person to be 'on'. Alternatively, suggest that children should hop or skip around.

40. Paper, scissors, stone

Challenge

Children line up opposite a partner, each standing in a hoop approximately one pace apart. After a joint count of three, the children select 'paper, scissors or stone'. The winners then have to run to a designated area before being tagged by their opponent.

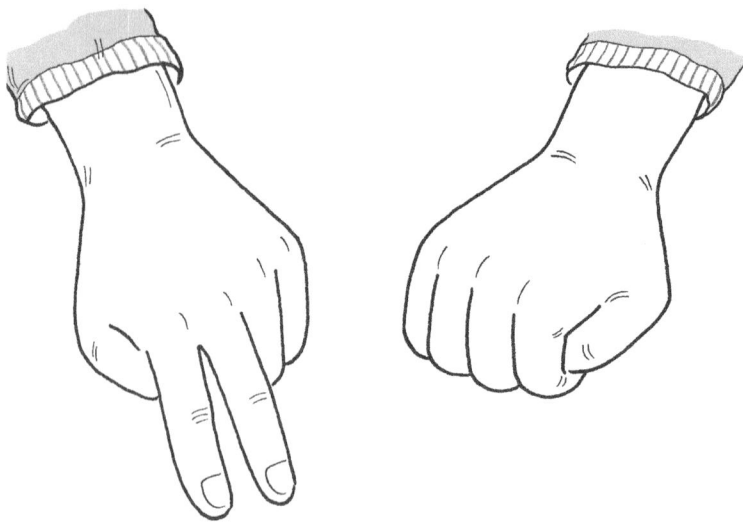

Tip
Arrange the children in two parallel lines, enabling them to easily progress to a different partner.

Development
Increasing the distance between pairings extends the length of pursuit.

41. Last hoop standing

Children stand in a circle, each holding a hoop on their left-hand-side. On the teacher's command, the children must let go of their own hoop and try to grab the hoop from the person on their right-hand-side. A child is eliminated if they fail to catch their neighbour's hoop before it falls flat.

Tip
Keeping the feet planted in the same position seems to help the children locate the hoop more successfully.

Development
When the children become practiced, they can try using just one hand, stand on one leg or face the opposite direction.

---

42. Hoop upsides again  ⭐☆

Teams of children stand in lines. Each team must transport a hoop from the front of their line to the back by stepping through it, in turn. The rear person in the line then runs to the front, and the process continues until the team manages to cross the finish line.

Tip
The optimal distance apart for team members to stand is a 'double' arm length, allowing hoops to be passed between team members.

Development
Children could complete ten star jumps or a similar activity each time they step through a hoop.

43. Olympic rings

Challenge

Teams race against each other over 'horizontal hurdles' to be the winning team.

Tip
Use medium-sized hoops, ensuring the leaps are easily incorporated into a smooth running style.

Development
Each team member must also complete a task after each 'leg', such as ten star jumps.

44. Table top

Challenge

Pairs of children collaborate to relay a cache of hoops from the start to the finishing line. They must proceed on all fours, balancing the hoop across their backs. Should the hoop fall off they must return to the start once more.

Tip
Each child should try to position themselves so they get the edge of the hoop in the middle of their backs – or alternatively the hoop can be positioned by a third team member.

Development
Encourage trios of children to try and transport two hoops in a similar fashion.

45. Outer circle

> **Challenge**
>
> Children are organised with the majority of the class on the outside of a circle of hoops, with several children remaining on the inside. The pupils inside the circle try to clear the hoops by rolling them in any direction, whilst the external players strive to return them before the circle is emptied.

Tip
Ensure that hoops are rolled away instead of thrown.

Development
Increasing or decreasing the size of the circle can make the challenge more competitive should one side be dominant.

46. Gold run

Challenge

Two teams compete against each other to cover a gap, positioning their hoops to allow them to stand holding hands. The child at the back of the line may run to reposition their hoop at the front before linking arms once more. The winning team is the first chain to cross over the finishing line.

Tip
A team can disrupt their opposition's progress by directing their chain across the intended course, enforcing a lengthy detour.

Development
Experiment with pairing competing teams with unequal numbers of members; is it beneficial to have greater or fewer team players?

47. The great escape

Children race in teams to cover a stipulated distance by taking it in turns to crawl through a tunnel. The tunnel is formed by team members positioning their hoops; the last person crawling through takes his place at the front of the tunnel thus facilitating forward progress.

Tip
The person crawling through the tunnel must leave their hoop with another team member; passing it along the line for retrieval when they emerge at the front.

Development
Use a variety of different sized hoops. Suggest that each of the hoops forming the tunnel must be placed three steps apart.

48. Tag team

Challenge

One child starts 'on'. They endeavour to tag another, and must then link with that child by holding onto the same hoop as they pursue the next person. Once a chain of four people (with three hoops) has been formed, the children split in to pairs and continue.

Tip
Hoops for linking the children should be easily accessible outside the designated playing area.

Development
Stipulate that children must only link with those who share certain criteria, the same colour of hair for instance.

---

49. Clockwork

Set out hoops to represent a clock face. Children race to the different hourly positions to stand in a hoop. The last person to reach the target time is eliminated from the game. An adjudicator calls out the times and determines who is 'out'.

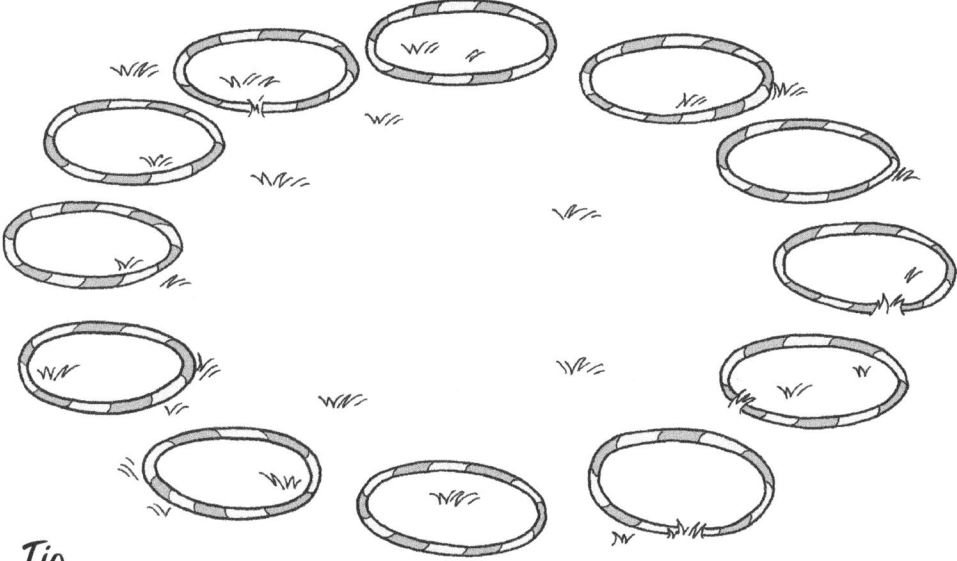

Tip
Ensure the circle is plenty large enough to encompass half-hourly times. Two adjacent circles would enable parallel games to take place simultaneously.

Development
Call out the times in 24 hour time, or give children simple calculations to consider; requiring them to visit more than one position around the clock face.

50. Boulder run

Challenge

Half the class form a 'corridor,' through which the other half endeavours to run. Hoops are rolled in the path of the runners, who must avoid them. The winner is the last person left 'in.'

Tip
All children must run along the corridor in the same direction; waiting before they begin the return journey.

Development
Adapt the length and width of the corridor accordingly.

Index (by level of difficulty)

Lightning Source UK Ltd.
Milton Keynes UK
UKOW06f0106270415

250388UK00001B/13/P